ID0603212

Writing Stories
Fairy Tales

Anita Ganeri

Heinemann
LIBRARY
Chicago, Illinois

© 2013 Heinemann Library
an imprint of Capstone Global Library, LLC
Chicago, Illinois

Edited by Dan Nunn, Rebecca Rissman, and Sian Smith
Designed by Joanna Hinton-Malivoire
Original illustrations © Capstone Global Library 2013
Picture research by Ruth Blair
Production by Sophia Argyris
Originated by Capstone Global Library Ltd
Printed and bound in China by South China Printing Company Ltd

ISBN: 978 1 4329 7531 9 (Hardback)
ISBN: 978 1 4329 7538 8 (Paperback)

17 16 15 14 13
10 9 8 7 6 5 4 3 2 1

Cataloging-in-Publication Data is available at the Library of Congress website.
Ganeri, Anita, 1961-
  Fairy tales / Anita Ganeri.
     p. cm.— (Writing stories)
  Includes bibliographical references and index.
  ISBN 978-1-4329-7531-9 (hb)—ISBN 978-1-4329-7538-8 (pb)
1. Fairy tales. 2. Creative writing. I. Title.

GR550.G294 2013
398.2—dc23   2012043114

Acknowledgments
We would like to thank the following for permission to reproduce photographs: Shutterstock background images and design features, pp.4 (© Thomas M Perkins), 6 (© notkoo), 7 (© advent), 8 (© jordache), 9 (© wavebreakmedia), 12 (© Kiselev Andrey Valerevich), 14 (© fcarucci), 16 (© nomeko), 16 (© VectorShots), 18 (© mikeledray), 22 (© Kirill__M), 24 (© EYUP IZZET CAGLAR), 26 (© Featureflash)

Cover photographs reproduced with permission of Shutterstock: castle (© Elena Schweitzer), rainbow (© Lori Giles), tree/flowers (© Mayovskyy Andrew), fairies (© AnastasijaD), crown (© Ivan Ponomarev), stars (© Flame of life).

Every effort has been made to contact copyright holders of material reproduced in this book. Any omissions will be rectified in subsequent printings if notice is given to the publisher.

All the Internet addresses (URLs) given in this book were valid at the time of going to press. However, due to the dynamic nature of the Internet, some addresses may have changed, or sites may have changed or ceased to exist since publication. While the author and publisher regret any inconvenience this may cause readers, no responsibility for any such changes can be accepted by either the author or the publisher.

Some words are shown in bold, **like this**. You can find out what they mean by looking in the glossary.

Contents

Follow this symbol to read a fairy tale.

Writing a Story

A story is a piece of **fiction** writing. It tells the reader about made-up people, places, and events. Anyone can write a story! What you need is a **setting**, some **characters**, and a **plot**.

You can write different types of stories. There are mystery stories, funny stories, adventure stories, scary stories, animal stories, and many others. This book is about writing fairy tales.

What Is a Fairy Tale?

A fairy tale is a **fictional** story. Many fairy tales have **characters** such as fairies, princesses, dragons, giants, and elves. Popular **settings** for fairy tales are castles and palaces, woods, or magical lands.

How many fairy tale characters do you recognize?

The **plot** of a fairy tale often tells of the struggle between two sides, such as good and evil, or rich and poor. A fairy tale usually has a happy ending. What is your favorite fairy tale?

Getting Ideas

Before you start writing, you need to get some ideas. Ideas may come from your imagination or from another fairy tale that you have read. You might start with an idea for an interesting **character** or an exciting twist to the **plot**.

A good way to remember your ideas is to jot them down in a notebook. Keep it with you all the time. Then you can scribble down anything that comes into your head, even if it is just a few words.

What's the Plot?

What happens in your fairy tale? This is called the **plot**. It needs a beginning, a middle, and an end. You can use a **story mountain**, like the one below, to help you plan your plot.

Middle
The main action happens. There may be a problem for one of your characters.

Beginning
Set the scene and introduce your main **character**.

Ending
The problem is solved and the story ends.

Your story starts at one side of the mountain, goes up to the top, then goes down the other side.

A **timeline** is another good way to figure out a plot. Mark the story's main events along the timeline. Here is a timeline for the fairy tale told in this book.

A princess forgets how to laugh.

⬇

The king tries everything to cheer her up.

⬇

A magician comes to the palace.

⬇

He tickles the princess with a feather. She laughs.

⬇

The magician is a prince in disguise.

⬇

The princess and prince fall in love.

⬇

The princess marries the prince.

Once Upon a Time

The beginning of your story is very important. This is where you introduce your main **character**. It needs to grab your readers' attention so that they want to keep reading.

Can you turn any of these ideas into story starters?

- A princess is put under a spell.
- A mermaid loses her magical shell.
- A giant falls down a bottomless well.

A Fairy Tale

Once upon a time, there lived
a princess. She was very pretty
and very kind. But she was
always sad. A wicked witch had
put a spell on her. The spell
made the princess forget how
to laugh.

 Many fairy tales start with "Once upon a time…"
Can you think of a different beginning?

Setting the Scene

Setting the scene means deciding on the place and time in which your story is set. It tells your reader where and when the story happens. A glittering palace, like the one below, makes a great **setting** for a fairy tale.

The princess lived in a glittering palace. The palace had dainty towers and turrets that soared into the sky. All around were pretty gardens filled with sweet-smelling flowers. It was the most beautiful place to live in the whole world.

Can you think of any other settings for your fairy tale?

Making Up Characters

Your story needs strong **characters** that your reader believes in and cares about. Think about what kind of people they are, what they look like, and how they are feeling. Jot down the details in fact files.

Character fact file
Character: Princess
Looks like: Pretty; long, dark hair
Sounds like: Musical voice
Personality: Kind; helpful
Likes: Kittens; cupcakes; pink shoes
Dislikes: Not being able to laugh

Character fact file
Character: Wicked witch
Looks like: Long, pointed nose; stringy hair
Sounds like: Mean, cackling voice
Personality: Cruel; vain
Likes: Toads; spells; herself
Dislikes: Pretty princesses

The princess and the wicked witch are the main characters in our story.

With her sparkling eyes and long, dark hair, the princess was the prettiest girl in the kingdom. She was also the kindest. Everybody loved her. Everybody, that is, except the wicked witch. The witch was old and cruel, and she hated the princess for being so nice.

Can you think up good names for the princess and the wicked witch?

17

The Middle

The middle of your story is where the main action happens. This is where something goes wrong for some of your **characters**, or they have to try to solve a tricky problem. Here are some problems that your fairy-tale characters might face.

The character...
- is turned into a frog
- gets lost in the woods
- falls into a deep sleep
- is tricked
- falls under a spell.

Can you think of any other problems?

The wicked witch hated the princess so much that she put her under a spell. The spell could only be broken if someone made the princess laugh.

"That'll show her," the witch cackled. "She won't look so pretty if she's always sad. No one will want to marry her now!"

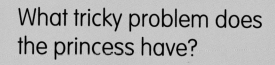
What tricky problem does the princess have?

Mind Mapping

It can be hard to think what happens next in your story. If you get stuck, try doing some **mind mapping** to help you move the **plot** along. Write down one key word or thought. Then jot down any connected words or thoughts that come into your head.

Don't spend too long on a mind map. A few minutes are enough.

giving her a kitten

putting on a funny show

What might cheer up the princess?

singing a silly song

tickling her with a feather

making the witch disappear

Everyone tried to make the princess laugh. The king gave her a kitten, but that didn't work. The queen sang her a silly song, but that didn't work, either. The princess's little sister put on a funny show. But nothing made the princess laugh.

Using Speech

Try using **dialogue** in your story. Dialogue means the words that people say. Dialogue shows what your **characters** are thinking and feeling. It helps bring your story to life.

"It's not working," sighed the king. "We'll just have to try something else."

Put **quotation marks** around the words that are spoken.

"It's not working," sighed the king. "We'll just have to try something else."

"But we've tried everything," said the queen, sadly. "What else can we do?"

The king put his head in his hands and thought hard.

"I know," he said. "I'll offer a reward to anyone who can make her laugh. That should do the trick."

 Dialogue is also good to break up long chunks of text.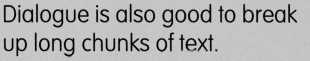

Exciting Writing

When you are describing your **characters** or **setting**, choose your words carefully. This will make your writing more exciting. You can add describing words called **adjectives** to explain what things are like, and **adverbs** to describe the way things are done.

Slowly, he pulled a large, purple feather from his sleeve.

Slowly is an adverb. *Large* and *purple* are adjectives.

One day, a magician arrived at the palace. He wore a dazzling coat of silver and gold. Slowly, he pulled a large, purple feather from his sleeve. He tickled the princess gently under her chin. The princess's mouth twitched. Then she smiled. Then she laughed a long, tinkling laugh.

How many adjectives and adverbs can you spot in the story?

Fairy-Tale Ending

You have reached the end of your story. This is the place where you need to tie up all the loose ends. The ending tells your reader what has happened to your **characters** and how they have solved any problems they had.

They all lived happily ever after.

Most fairy tales end happily and the characters' wishes come true.

The spell was broken! Now, the princess couldn't stop laughing. Her family was delighted. The king offered the magician a reward.

"I'd like to marry the princess," said the magician, who was really a handsome prince in disguise.

The princess said yes at once. So, the prince and princess got married and lived happily ever after.

 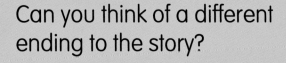Can you think of a different ending to the story?

More Top Tips

1 Read lots of fairy tales by other writers. This will help to spark ideas and give you a good feel for this type of story writing.

2 Read your story out loud to see if it sounds right. This can be particularly helpful when you are writing **dialogue**.

3 Be ready to rewrite your story several times before you are completely happy with it. This is what lots of writers do.

4 Try making a **story mountain** using a well-known fairy tale, such as *Little Red Riding Hood*. This will help you plan your own story.

5 Tell your story from a different point of view to make it more interesting. For example, you could use the princess's voice.

6 Even though you are writing a fairy tale, make your **characters** believable. Put yourself in their shoes and think about what you would do or say.

Glossary

adjective describing word that tells you about a noun (a noun is a naming word)

adverb describing word that tells you about a verb (a verb is a doing word)

character person in a piece of writing

dialogue words that characters say

fiction piece of writing that is about made-up places, events, and characters

fictional about made-up places, events, and characters

mind mapping thinking of everything you can about a subject

plot what happens in a story

quotation marks marks that show the words someone has spoken

setting time and place in which a story is set

story mountain mountain-shaped diagram that helps you plan out a story

timeline list of events in the order in which they happen

Find Out More

Books

Ganeri, Anita. *Writing Stories*. Chicago: Raintree, 2013.

Stowell, Louie, and Jane Chisholm. *Write Your Own Story Book*. Tulsa, Okla.: EDC, 2011.

Warren, Celia. *How to Write Stories* (How to Write). Laguna Hills, Calif.: QEB, 2007.

Web sites

Facthound offers a safe, fun way to find Internet sites related to this book. All of the sites on Facthound have been researched by our staff.

Here's all you do:
Visit **www.facthound.com**
Type in this code: 9781432975319.

Index